FRENCH REVOLUTION

A History From Beginning To End

Copyright © 2016 by Hourly History.

Table of Contents

Chapter One

An Environment of Revolution

"Freedom is a gift from heaven, and every individual of the same species has the right to enjoy it as soon as he is in enjoyment of his reason."

—Denis Diderot

During the late years of the eighteenth century, the spirit of Enlightenment thinking and revolution were in the air. The world was changing—moving away from ingrained beliefs about religion, reason, society, and the rights of the individual and turning towards the laws of nature as interpreted by the scientific method. Nowhere was the influence of this radical new way of thinking more apparent than in France, and the upheaval it caused would come to bloody fruition in the form of revolution.

The Age of Enlightenment, also known as the Age of Reason and the Siecle des Lumieres in French, began slowly in the late seventeenth century and then spread to the height of its popularity in the eighteenth century when Enlightenment ideas became common topics in social clubs and meeting places throughout Europe. The world of science had gone through its own revolution, moving toward empirical observation and the scientific method and away from religious dogma and the structure of absolute monarchy. The work of Copernicus' "De revoltionibus orbium coelestium," or "On the Revolutions of the Heavenly Spheres," Galileo Galilei's "Dialogue Concerning the Two Chief World Systems," and Isaac Newton's "Philosophiae Naturalis Principia Mathematica," or "Mathematical Principles of Natural Philosophy," described natural truths that gave the world constants and predictability where before were mystery and prophecy. Philosophers like John Locke brought "natural law" into societal discourse in his "Essay Concerning Human Understanding," and Thomas Hobbes, in his "Leviathan," wrote of the nature of equality and the natural state of mankind and championed reforms of government. In France, publications by Enlightenment thinkers, like Voltaire's "On Tolerance," Rousseau's "Emile," Montesquieu's "De l'Espirit des Lois," Comte Buffon's "L'Histoire Naturalle," and Diderot's "On the Interpretation of Nature," spoke about religious and political freedoms as well as views on the nature of humanity and the equality of all men. Rousseau, in particular, argued against the long-held belief that monarchs ruled by divine right with his work "The Social Contract", saying, "Let us then admit that force does not create right, and that we are obliged to obey only legitimate powers," which would have great influence in the years to come.

Across the Atlantic, Enlightenment thinking had inspired the thirteen American colonies to revolt against

British rule by refusing to abide by taxation passed without representation among other injustices. As a political writer, who borrowed heavily from European Enlightenment writers like John Locke, Thomas Jefferson wrote the American Declaration of Independence and even the new American Constitution wrote of Enlightenment ideas as the foundation of society. Benjamin Franklin—author, philosopher, and inventor—was another leader of the American Revolution. His views on social structure, including such phrases as "Rebellion to tyrants is obedience to God," and "They who can give up essential liberty to obtain a little temporary safety deserve neither liberty nor safety," made him a popular figure in France when he visited as America's diplomatic representative to secure aid from the French government. The French monarchy contributed more than a billion livres, troops, and naval support to support the American Revolution. It is assumed that this generosity was based in large part on King Louis XVI's hatred for England after the English took over most of France's colonial territories, including Canada, France's foothold in the New World, in the Seven Years War. Another motivating factor was the possible recovery of those territories should the Americans prove successful. An army of French soldiers and a large French naval fleet would play deciding roles in the American struggle for independence, particularly the French naval blockade against the dominant British navy and the French forces that took part in the eventual British surrender at Yorktown. The American Revolution, which came to its conclusion in 1781 with the rebellious

American colonists victorious against the might of the British army, was an amazing upset of world power. This victory, resulting in a government based on popular sovereignty, provided a solid example of the power of the common citizen to make societal changes, even against staggering odds. The parallels to the situation in France were obvious; common people revolting against a powerful king whose rule denied them the rights they felt God had given them. The language used in the American Declaration of Independence, which enumerated the reasons colonists felt it was their duty to revolt and how life, liberty, and the pursuit of happiness were rights due to all men equally, as well as the example of successful revolution were well received by the French citizens who were struggling under the inept and extravagant rule of King Louis XVI.

Beyond the money and the expenses of providing personnel, military and naval support to support the American revolutionaries, the French treasury was severely strained by the losses sustained during the Seven Years War, as well as the exorbitant debt incurred by the monarchy during the reign of the king's father and his grandfather, who had spared no expense redesigning the royal hunting lodge in the forest around Versailles into one of the largest palaces in the world simply because he wanted to get away from the stress of life at the palace in Paris. The new queen, Marie Antoinette of Austria, was a young girl who understood little about the people she came to rule. She was flamboyant and extravagant, spending lavishly on dresses and jewelry. Even her extreme hairstyles, piled high and decorated with elements like miniature ships, fruit, and jewels, became a symbol to the people of France of the utter disconnect between their lives and the lives of their rulers. Her expenditures were a visible drain on an already struggling economy and garnered ill will from her destitute subjects. In fact, she became known in Paris as "Madame Deficit." It did not help her image that in four years of marriage, she had not yet produced an heir to the throne, which was considered the purpose of a queen. Although it had been proven that the King suffered from a medical condition that was the true cause of the barren marriage, this was not something that was explained to the common people. After the King underwent a necessary surgery, the couple was able to conceive and eventually have four children, including the heir to the throne, Louis Joseph.

The tense situation was only exacerbated when bad weather and poor harvests in the mid-1780s caused a food shortage. Most damaging was the shortage of bread, which was the main source of food for the poor peasants of France. It was the traditional responsibility of the king to make sure the peasants had an adequate supply. Because of this, the king was often called "le premier boulanger du royaume," or "the prime baker of the kingdom." During this period of food shortage, grain merchants were viewed with suspicion by the hungry citizenry. They were called the "most cruel enemies of the people," because it was believed they hoarded grain and mixed in other substances, such as crushed bone meal and chalk, in order to inflate their profits. In response to the scarcity of bread, noble houses and country estates were attacked and looted by hungry citizens in search of food with alarming frequency. These riots by peasants living in the French country were known as "la Grand Peur" or the Great Fear. Food prices soared as supply was even scarcer and the overtaxed citizens of the Third Estate, which made up ninety-eight percent of the total population, were starving and angry. Change was inevitable, and when it came, it was terrifying.

Chapter Two

The Estates

"Freedom is the alone unoriginated birthright of man, and belongs to him by force of his humanity."

—Immanuel Kant

France, during this period and indeed for centuries past, was a society based on the feudal system and was organized into three estates. This division was set up along the ancient lines of "those who pray, those who fight, and those who work."

The first estate consisted of the clergy, including all churches and all of the king's clerics. The clergy was exempt from paying any taxes due to their religious standing. Citizens were required to pay a tenth of their income to the church as tithes that maintained the lifestyle of the First Estate. Local churches remained poor as funds were sent on to church leaders in Paris, so the people knew their money was not being used in their communities.

The Second Estate consisted of France's aristocracy, those considered to be of noble birth. This group also did not pay taxes, except during wartime, and even then it was usually not enforced. As many in the aristocracy were also landlords and owners of mills, wine presses, and bakeries, the common people were required to pay rent on land they farmed and taxes on the equipment they used, and this money maintained the lifestyle of the members of the Second Estate.

The Third Estate included merchants, artisans, peasants, and all the rest of the working class. This group carried most of the tax burden of the nation. In difficult times when harvests were poor, the taxes were devastating and peasants would often starve to death during a harsh winter. The system set up rigid classes of people and allowed for very little mobility. Generally, a person was expected to live as a member of the class into which they were born. Members of the Third Estate were blocked from holding even the lowest position of power in government that would allow them to improve quality of life. It was also impossible for the Third Estate to make changes within the law to better their situation, because the first two Estates together held the power to overrule any changes that would negatively affect their wealth and power. With the guidance of Enlightenment thinking, the members of the Third Estate were beginning to realize the system needed to be changed in order for their lives to change.

With the economy in ruins and the countryside in a state of unrest, Louis XVI was forced to take action. In 1786, Charles Alexandre de Calonne, the Controller-General, suggested a solution that involved major financial reform through a universal land tax that did not exempt the upper classes—an action that was extremely unpopular with the powerful nobility. Because it was necessary to bring in greater taxes from somewhere and the clergy and nobility were resistant, the King appointed men of non-noble origin as his finance ministers. One of these commoners, Jacques Necker was popular with the people because he proposed many reforms to the tax laws that would help lift some of the burden on the citizenry, specifically attempts to reduce the expenses of the court. Unfortunately, most of his reform efforts failed.

As a further step in the plan to deal with the worsening economic situation and public unrest, the King summoned the Estates General; a group of representatives from all three classes of society, the clergy, the nobility, and the non-aristocratic Third Estate, which had not met in over a hundred years. The meeting took place in May 1789 at the Palace of Versailles. The representatives came prepared with lists of grievances to be addressed by the assembly. All three pushed for reforms to economic and judicial policies, reflecting the general depression in the economy, but the Third Estate wanted major policy changes, including equal representation in government as opposed to the upper classes having all the power and none of the tax burden.

Predictably, the three groups could not agree on reforms that would take power and privilege away from the clergy and aristocracy. Frustrated by the stalemate, the Third Estate met separately and formed the National Assembly to formulate their goals for the meeting of the Estates General. They took on the task of writing a new constitution for France, based on Enlightenment ideas of equality, and invited the other two groups to contribute.

Many in the clergy and even some of the nobility joined in seeking greater societal reform. A few days into this process, the King, concerned by the direction the National Assembly was heading, especially with regard to taxes, ordered the building they had been using as a discussion space to be locked in an attempt to block the meeting. The group rightly feared that this was a precursor to ending the meeting of the Estates General without effecting any changes. Denied their meeting hall, the National Assembly gathered in a an indoor tennis court nearby and took what would become to be known as the "Tennis Court Oath," vowing not to disband, even if the King ended the formal assembly of the Estates General, until they had achieved the constitutional reform they championed. Because many of the representatives of the clergy and the nobility joined the cause, King Louis was forced to continue the assembly of the Estates General, but now restructured and repurposed as the new National Assembly.

Chapter Three

Rise of the Third Estate

"The secret of freedom lies in educating people, whereas the secret of tyranny is in keeping them ignorant."

—Maximilien Robespierre

The people of Paris became convinced that a royalist military attack to destabilize the National Assembly was imminent. As a reaction to the National Assembly's refusal to disperse when ordered, King Louis XVI began deploying troops in large numbers around Paris and Versailles. Even some foreign regiments were brought in to support the King's own forces. When the National Assembly requested the removal of the troops, Louis responded haughtily that troop deployment was his purview and assured the representatives that their presence was simply a precautionary measure. The Parisian citizens were convinced they would need to act in order to protect themselves and the progress being made by the National Assembly. Adding to the environment of distrust, the King dismissed Jacques Necker, the popular finance minister, on July 12th after he suggested a tax on the first two Estates. This left the Third Estate feeling that their voice in the government was gone.

The people were outraged and took to the streets in increasingly violent riots. In particular, gun shops, small armories, and private collections throughout Paris were looted for armaments to prepare for the fight to come. The citizens even ransacked and destroyed forty of the fifty-four government customs posts in the city. On July 14, 1789, a group of citizens stormed the Hotel des Invalides in western Paris and acquired some thirty thousand rifles, and even some small artillery pieces, but little gunpowder to load them with. Officers of military regiments stationed nearby who were sympathetic to the peasants' cause refused to intervene to protect the hotel. In fact, a deserting guardsman even informed the crowd of the large store of gunpowder that was currently being housed in the Bastille, a royal prison used to house political prisoners, some two miles away in the neighborhood of Faubourg Saint Antoine. The crowd responded by marching through the streets, hauling their rifles and cannon, in order to storm the Bastille and take its supply of gunpowder. Upon their arrival at the fortress, the crowd attempted to negotiate with the commander of the guard force for the gunpowder. When representatives tried to enter the fortress to negotiate, Bastille guards fired on the crowd, killing hundreds of the rioters. This attack by the French military on the people's representatives caused outrage among the mob, and the crowd laying siege to the Bastille swelled to even greater numbers as citizens arrived from throughout the city in support. When soldiers who were sent to disperse the mob and defend the Bastille arrived, two detachments of the guard instead joined the crowd in the attack on the fortress. The common people had not known how to use the canons they had acquired and dragged through the streets, so the arrival of the experienced soldiers was a major boon. After a few hours, the defenders were defeated. When the Bastille's commander, the Marquis de Launay, surrendered, the people entered and killed the guards. The commander was beheaded, possibly by a baker using a small bread knife, and his head was placed on a pike and paraded around the city as a symbol of the victory. That night, some eight hundred victorious citizens tore down the walls of the prison, seeing it as a symbol of royal absolutism and the oppression they were fighting against, and seven prisoners were freed. France celebrates July 14th as Bastille Day and views it as the beginning of the Revolution.

Ironically, in the King's diary on that date is a simple entry: "nothing." Although this comment was meant to refer to the results of his hunting excursion that day, it is obvious that the King had very little understanding of the concerning state of French society.

Chapter Four

The Rights of Man

"Man is born free and everywhere he is in chains."

—Jean Jacques Rousseau

On August 4th, 1789, less than a month after the Bastille was taken, the National Assembly adopted the Declaration of the Rights of Man and the Citizen. This document was a statement of the revolutionaries' goals that included a list of the individual and collective rights due to all men equally. It was influenced heavily by Enlightenment ideals and the writings of Jean Jacques Rousseau, who is often called the " Father of the Revolution." It also borrowed from the recent documents of the American Revolution, including the Declaration of Independence and the Constitution of the United States. The French declaration was presented to the National Assembly by General Gilbert du Motier, Marquis de Lafayette, who had played a major role in fighting the American Revolution. While composing the proposed declaration, he sought input from his friend Thomas Jefferson, writer of the American documents. The document approved by the National Assembly laid out seventeen points of what they believed to be "the natural, inalienable, and sacred rights of man. They included equality, with distinctions between citizens based only on "public utility;" liberty; property; security; resistance to oppression; equal access opportunity without regard for social status; protection from arrest, unless it be a result of breaking a law, civil punishments established by law; the concept that citizens were to be presumed innocent until proven guilty; freedom of expression; a police force beholden to the people and not for the personal benefit of public officials paid for by a general tax that applied to all citizens; accountability to society for any public agents; proscribed separation of legal powers in government; and the right to property.

By declaring the natural rights of man and making no mention of the role of the monarchy, the National Assembly effectively abolished the feudal system that had been in place in France for hundreds of years, and at the same time, the long-held rights of the nobility provided by the feudal system. Freedoms of speech and of the press were declared as important policies of the new government and were championed by radical lawyer, Maximilien Robespierre. The adoption of the Declaration of the Rights of Man and the Citizen was a potent first step in the ultimate goal of crafting a new constitution that reformed the French system of government.

Chapter Five

Writers and Reformers

"To show how much we have become slaves, it is enough just to cast a glance on the capital and examine the morals of its inhabitants."

—Jean Paul Marat

In particular, one reform to the judicial system made by the National Assembly was to have a far-reaching effect on the Revolution in the years to come. There was to be one form of execution for all criminals, regardless of their social standing. Previously, common people were often executed on the breaking wheel, which had originally been designed as a torture device, or they were hanged. Beheading via axe or sword was a method of execution reserved for condemned aristocrats as it was thought to be less painful and more dignified, even though it often required multiple strikes from the headsman before the head was removed and the execution complete. Dr. Joseph Ignace Guillotin, himself an opponent of capital punishment, recommended several changes to the practice of execution, including that all condemned criminals, regardless of status or crime, would be executed humanely in the same manner. He suggested an execution machine, based on the English Halifax Gibbet and the

Scottish Maiden. It was a mechanism consisting of a tall, upright frame fit with a suspended weighted blade. The condemned prisoner was secured in stocks at the base of the frame and positioned directly under the blade. When the blade was released, it would fall with the force of gravity and decapitate the victim in one blow. Then known in France as a louisette, it was viewed as a less painful and more consistent means of execution. The device was adopted, and though it was often called the "People's Razor" because of the many public executions of the convicted "enemies of the people," it soon became associated with the man who suggested it and has been known as the guillotine ever since, standing as a grim symbol of the Revolution.

Taking firm hold of the newly championed freedom of the press, one journalist became famous as the voice of the people during the Revolution. Jean Paul Marat was an accomplished physician, scientist, and writer. At one time, he held the position of court doctor to the French aristocrats, making it all the more extraordinary when he turned his back on his life of privilege and became instrumental in calling for many of his former clients' deaths via the guillotine. Marat turned all of his energy toward the cause of the Revolution and particularly, the rights of the "sans-culottes," a slang name for the common people of Paris who wore full-length trousers instead of the culottes, or knee breaches, favored by the aristocracy. In September 1789, Marat started his own paper, called L'Ami du peuple, or The Friend of the People. His writings in this popular paper were radical and controversial and aggressively attacked some of the most powerful people and groups in France. He often called for violence against any he believed to be enemies of the Revolution.

At the time of the Revolution, Marat had suffered for several years with a skin disease that caused him to spend much of his time soaking in a medicinal bath. He wrote many of his articles for L'Ami du peuple using a board placed across the bath as his writing desk. Marat's words had such powerful effect inciting the mob violence and executions of the Terror that a young woman from nearby Caen, Charlotte Corday, saw him as the main cause for the terrible violence gripping France. Mademoiselle Corday came to Paris in July 1793 with the express purpose of murdering the man whose work she blamed for the deaths of so many others. She found Marat in his bath and pretended to have brought a list of enemies of the Revolution in Caen for Marat to expose in his paper. Upon his response that those on the list would see the guillotine within the week, she proceeded to fatally stab him in the chest with a kitchen knife that she had concealed inside her dress. She made no attempt to escape but calmly faced her arrest and following trial, where she stated, "I killed one man to save a hundred thousand." She was guillotined three days after the murder. The murdered journalist, physician, and self-proclaimed friend of the people was mourned in Paris. He came to be viewed as something of a saint for the Revolution with people going so far as to replace crucifixes in churches with busts of Marat. One of the most famous artists of the period Jacques Louis David even painted a romanticized version of the scene of Marat's death. In the painting, the murdered man's body is posed specifically in a manner reminiscent of early representations of the passion of Christ. Jean Paul Marat had become a martyr to the cause of the Revolution.

Another writer who responded to the Declaration of the Rights of Man and the Citizen was feminist Olympe de Gouges. De Gouges was a successful playwright and activist in Paris. Disappointed that the National Assembly had denied female citizens the right to equality that was such a cornerstone of the natural rights of men, as well as the emphasis on "fraternite" as part of the foundation for the hoped-for new society, she wrote and published her own declaration in 1791. The Declaration of the Rights of Women and the Female Citizen followed the points in the Declaration of the Rights of Man and the Citizen published by the National Assembly in a style that was almost a parody of the original document. It began with its dedication to Queen Marie Antoinette, naming her "the most hated woman in all of Europe," and continues with a call to the men of France and the spirit of the Revolution. "Man, are you capable of being fair? A woman is asking: at least you will allow her that right. Tell me? What gave you the sovereign right to oppress my sex?" She demanded the same rights so recently expressed as inalienable rights of man as also due to women, using much the same arguments used to support the various rights for men. Beyond this, Olympe de Gouges also spoke out for all who had been left out of the promise of equality, including women and slaves. Her plays spread the ideas of women's rights and the rights of black slaves throughout Europe and even into the newly created United States of America. Because her writing was critical of the National Assembly, even though supportive of their ideas, she was accused of treason. She was convicted and executed along with many other so-called "enemies of the state" by guillotine during the period of the Reign of Terror.

Chapter Six

Captives in Paris

"Laws are the sovereigns of sovereigns."

—Louis XIV

On the fifth of October, soon after the Declaration of the Rights of Man and the Citizen was adopted, an angry mob of Parisian women, mostly Parisian fishwives who had ironically been labeled by the National Assembly as "passive citizens" and thus denied the equality promoted by the Declaration, marched on the royal palace at Versailles, demanding bread. These women actually entered the palace and attempted to murder the queen. Upon arrival of the Garde nationale led by Lafayette, the rioting woman were brought to a compromise and the entire royal family was escorted by the mob back to Paris where they were installed in the Tuileries Palace. It was felt that the King would be more accountable to the people if he lived in the city as opposed to the country estate of Versailles outside of Paris. In reality, the King and his family were prisoners in the palace, surrounded by the hostile people they had so recently ruled. In June 1791, King Louis XVI and his family attempted to escape Paris, dressed as commoners. They intended to seek sanctuary in Austria, with hopes of garnering support and eventually reclaiming the power of the throne. It became obvious that the popularity of the Revolution was far more widespread than the King believed when the royal family was recognized in the town of Varennes-en-Argonne and not only denied the proper respect but forcibly returned under guard to house arrest in the Tuileries.

The royal family's ill-fated escape attempt caused upheaval in the already deeply troubled nation. The people now had proof that the King was set against the ideas of governmental reform called for by the National Assembly. The attempt and plans for recapturing France revealed by letters and other documents discovered in the King's room were seen as treason against the nation and her people. He had intended to abandon the country in the people's greatest hour of need. The King, whose role in government had become increasingly unnecessary with the changes he had been forced to accept from the Assembly, was now viewed as an enemy of the people.

This treatment of the monarch had other royalty around Europe understandably upset. In August, the Holy Roman Emperor Leopold II, who was also Queen Marie Antoinette's brother, along with Prussian ruler King Frederick William II put forth the Declaration of Pillnitz. This document supported the French royal family and threatened severe consequences to France if they were harmed. It also encouraged other European monarchies to join in aiding the French crown. Although this gesture and threat of reprisal had been meant as a safeguard for the beleaguered royals, it was seen by revolutionary leaders in Paris as an attempt by a foreign government to take over part of the governance of France, causing suspicion and paranoia to rise.

While European powers took stances against the French revolutionary government, France's former allies in the newly recognized United States of America watched the developments in France. At first, most Americans were enthusiastic about the rumors of political change. They were obviously sympathetic with the French citizens' desire for liberty and equality based on their own experiences, and it was hoped that France would develop into a republican ally in world affairs, particularly against the British monarchy. However, as the political instability and violence grew in France, many Americans became frightened. Though the decision was controversial, America remained neutral in France's struggle against European coalition forces.

Chapter Seven

Vive la Revolution!

"Allons enfants de la Patrie,

Le jour de gloire est arrivé!

Contre nous de la tyrannie,

L'etendard sanglant est leve."

—La Marseillaise

In the spring of 1792, the newly elected Legislative Assembly declared war on Austria and Prussia, responding in part to the threatening tone of the Declaration of Pillnitz. It was believed that a large number of royalists and other enemies of the Revolution had fled to Austria and were planning an attack of their own. The Legislative Assembly was also hoping to forestall the enemies of the Revolution overall, unify the people of France against an external enemy, and spread the ideas of the Revolution throughout Europe. Queen Marie Antoinette seemed to confirm the Legislative Assembly's fears of Austria's determination to reinstate the monarchy as she wrote in her diary, "The ministers and the Jacobins are making the king declare war tomorrow on Austria.

The ministers are hoping that this move will frighten the Austrians and that within three weeks we will be negotiating May we at last be avenged for all the outrages we have suffered from this country!"

With the new citizen government now at the head of a revolution in their own country and a foreign war, the attempt at managing the French effort was confused and chaotic. The French military was spread thin and at first fared poorly against their powerful adversaries. When coalition armies invaded France on April 25th, the mayor of Strasbourg requested his friend Claude Joseph Rouget de Lisle compose a battle song for the French army. That night, perhaps inspired by the foreign army so near, he wrote the song originally called "Chant de guerre pour l'Armee du Rhin," or, in English, "War Song for the Army of the Rhine". This song, with its stirring call to protect the homeland, soon became the anthem of the French Revolution. The name was changed after a group of volunteer citizen soldiers from Marseille sang it as they marched into Paris to join the revolutionary forces there. "La Marseillaise" was adopted as the national anthem of France until Napoleon took power. The song was reinstated in 1879 and remains the French national anthem to this day.

Not long after, in September 1792, the French military at last achieved their first major victory and pushed back an invasion of allied Austrian and Prussian forces near the northern town of Valmy. After being cut off from their supply lines by some clever maneuvers on the part of the French army, the Prussian infantry forces found themselves in a battle with the canons of a well-placed French division. When the Prussian line seemed to have reached a standstill, the French forces joined together in shouting, "Vive la nation" and singing "La Marseillaise." Unexpectedly, and seemingly miraculously to the French, the Prussian army broke off the attack and left the field. The invading force managed a hasty circuitous retreat and was pushed back well beyond the border of Rhine river. The famous German writer Johann Wolfgang von Goethe was with the Prussian army and witnessed the rout. Writing about the event, Goethe stated to his comrades, "From this place, and from this day forth begins a new era in the history of the world, and you can all say that you were present at its birth." Indeed, the French army did take full advantage of the change in the tide of war. The retreat of the Austrian and Prussian army allowed French forces to push into Germany and Belgium and capture important territories there.

In 1793, several more nations became involved in the war. Spain, the United Provinces, and Great Britain joined Austria and Prussia in the First Coalition against the French Revolutionary government. The Legislative Assembly responded to this by declaring a levy en masse, meaning all Frenchmen were to be at the disposal of the French army. This tactic allowed the French to raise large armies quickly in order to fight off the impressive group of powers arrayed against them. The armies that took the field were in fact, larger than those typically seen in Europe up to this point.

King Louis XVI and Marie Antoinette, who had been watching their power and privilege erode by the acts of the rebellious citizenry, must have been hopeful initially that France's defeat in the Assembly's war might work in their favor and return them to rule. This hope became more desperate with the repeated success of the revolutionary forces against the coalition forces and was definitely quashed when extremist Jacobin insurgents attacked the Tuileries Palace in Paris and placed the king under arrest on August 13, 1793.

Chapter Eight

Royal Trial

"We swear to exterminate every single criminal who wants to rob us of happiness and liberty."

—Maximilien Robespierre

The King and his family were taken and housed in the Temple. This was an ancient fortress prison in Paris built by the famed Knights Templar during the thirteenth century to serve as their headquarters in Europe. In the month that followed, revolutionaries in Paris massacred hundreds of Parisian citizens accused of being traitors to the Revolution. In September 1794, emboldened by military success and the arrest of Louis XVI, the Legislative Assembly formally abolished the monarchy and declared France to be a Republic. On December 11th, the King was indicted for high treason and over thirty individual crimes against the state, including his forced suspension of the meeting of the National Assembly that had brought about the Tennis Court Oath, his attempt to disperse the National Assembly under threat of the military, his attempt to intimidate citizens and the members of the National Assembly with the build-up of military power around Paris, his delays in recognizing the Declaration of the Rights of Man among other reforms passed by the National Assembly, his attempt to build a response among the citizens of France against revolutionary ideas, his failed attempt to escape France with his family against the will of the people, his attempts to bribe members of the military to act on his behalf instead of on the behalf of the people, his failure to repudiate the Declaration of Pillnitz which represented the goal of reinstating the monarchy in France, the attack by French troops on the people of Marseilles who had been involved in subduing counter-revolutionaries, his conspiring with his brothers to undermine the revolutionary government including an attempt to supply French troops to aid in their plot, his failure to provide adequate defense for France against her enemies, his strategy of foreign diplomacy that had the goal of weakening France and strengthening her enemies, his placing of counter-revolutionary officials in key appointments in order to undermine the National Assembly, his weakening of the French naval forces by allowing passports to many of the officers wishing to leave the service, his favoritism toward loyalist portions of the population, his suspension of a lawful decree passed by the National Assembly regarding the clergy, his maintenance of the Swiss Guards as his personal body guard in spite of the order by the National Assembly that they be disbanded, his failure to exact reparation for the disgrace experienced by the French at the hands of Spain, Germany, and Italy, and most damning, his actions that "caused the blood of Frenchmen to flow."

With all of these charges laid to his account, letters in the king's own hand, correspondence with other European monarchies, and witnesses to his crimes were entered into evidence. It was overwhelmingly clear to the representatives of the National Assembly that the King was not a supporter of the revolutionary government or the reforms that were being attempted by the National Assembly. In this way, he was acting against the interests of the French citizens and so the accusation of treason was upheld. In many of the instances cited in the list of charges, it seems Louis was only acting for his own self-preservation and that of his family and against what was obviously a violent uprising, but to the fervent idealists of the National Assembly, these were crimes against the progress of liberty.

He was addressed during the trial as "Citizen Louis Capet," indicating his reduced station. The King's lawyer, Raymond Deseze, spoke for three hours in front of the assembly in the King's defense, addressing all of the charges and painting Louis as a "friend of the people." Louis himself stated in his own defense, "I have always acted from my love of the people." Not one of the representatives voted against the guilty verdict passed on January 14th, although some abstained. Through the following two days, arguments were made as to the punishment that should be administered for Louis' crimes. The first vote cast was also the first vote that called for Louis' immediate execution. Predictably, it was Maximilien Robespierre who voted, saying, "The sentiment that led me to call for the abolition of the death penalty is the same that today forces me to demand that it be applied to the tyrant of my country." Even Louis' own cousin and former duke of Orleans, Philippe Egalite, voted for the death sentence. The final vote was extremely close, with many delegates preferring imprisonment or exile, but ultimately it came out in favor of executing the king. The 21st of January was set as the date of the execution.

On the morning of the execution, Louis was dressed and prepared by his former manservant. He visited a priest for confession and heard a last mass. The King was then conveyed from the Temple prison to the Place de la Revolution in a green carriage, which he shared with a priest and two guards. The carriage was accompanied by drummers playing loudly and a cavalry troop carrying drawn swords in order to guard against any possible rescue attempts by loyalists. An ill-fated attempt was made, but so many of the conspirators were already under arrest for other charges that the few remaining were soon killed with little disruption to the procession. The route was lined with soldiers of the National Guard and supporters of the Revolution holding back the crowd. The King was described as having mounted the platform bravely and allowing himself to be strapped down. When the heavy blade fell, many in the crowd rushed forward to catch some of the King's blood with their handkerchiefs as a souvenir.

High executioner of the First French Republic, Charles Henri Sanson, who executed over three thousand people during his career, described the scene on the day he carried out the execution of the king:

Arriving at the foot of the guillotine, Louis XVI looked for a moment at the instruments of his execution and asked Sanson why the drums had stopped beating. He came forward to speak, but there were shouts to the executioners to get on with their work. As he was strapped down, he exclaimed, "My people, I die innocent!" Then, turning towards his executioners, Louis XVI declared, "Gentlemen, I am innocent of everything of which I am accused. I hope that my blood may cement the good fortune of the French." The blade fell. It was January 21, 1793, 10:22 am. One of the assistants showed the head of Louis XVI to the people, whereupon a huge cry of "Vive la Nation! Vive la République!" arose and an artillery salute rang out which reached the ears of the imprisoned Royal family.

The execution of Louis XVI was the first time a monarch had been tried and executed by his own people. The King was dead; long live the Revolution. There was no turning back.

Chapter Nine

Reign of Terror

"Terror is the order of the day."

—Maximilien Robespierre

Following Louis XVI's execution, the Legislative Assembly struggled once more with internal divisions among its members. They did not unanimously approve the extremity of the action that had been taken and the course that had been set. The Jacobins were the radical group fiercely protective of the gains of the Revolution. They took their name from their meeting place, a convent previously used by the Dominicans whom Parisians commonly referred to as Jacobins. The Jacobins soon took prominence in the Assembly over the moderate Girondins. The Girondins had campaigned for the end of the monarchy but felt the Revolution had lost course. They called for a return to the original causes of the rebellion.

The Jacobins wanted to create a new society, free from the influence of past power structures. They established a new calendar no longer based on Christian dates. This included a ten-day week to negate the importance of Sundays and new names for the months, which were based on natural phenomena through the seasons. One of the leaders of this group was Maximilien Robespierre who famously said, "The king must die so that the country can live." He is also credited as having coined the phrase, "liberte, egalite, fraternite" in one of his early speeches. This was a common saying during the Revolution, as it expressed the goals put forth by the common people and later became the national motto of France. Robespierre was so dedicated to the principles of the Revolution and the rights of the people that he became known as "the Incorruptible." His persistence in defending equal rights for all men, along with his impassioned fiery speeches, gained great popularity and power with the citizens of France. Robespierre's rise to power led to what became known as the Reign of Terror: ten months during which thousands of suspected enemies of the revolution were executed via the guillotine. Robespierre encouraged the blood-thirst as a means of achieving a virtuous society. He likened terror itself to necessary virtue in his speeches"

If the basis of popular government in peacetime is virtue, the basis of popular government during a revolution is both virtue and terror; virtue, without which terror is baneful; terror, without which virtue is powerless. Terror is nothing more than speedy, severe and inflexible justice; it is thus an emanation of virtue; it is less a principle in itself, than a consequence of the general principle of democracy, applied to the most pressing needs of the patrie.

The violence became extreme to the point that failing to wear tricolor ribbons showing support for the Revolution or even using the wrong form of address—the outdated Madame or Monsieur instead of the new title, "Citizen,"—when speaking was justification for immediate arrest and execution. The mob now saw popular violence as a political right and thus an immediate expression of patriotism. One of the worst moments of this violent expression was the prison massacre that occurred in September 1792. A mob of citizens dragged around two thousand prisoners, including priests and nuns, from their cells and summarily executed them. The National Convention disapproved of this level of violence from the citizenry but continued with violence and execution and only sham trials as a legitimate instrument of government.

As the death toll rose, public executions became a popular event with the citizens of Paris. They were considered entertainment, attracting large crowds to the renamed Place Louis XV, now called the Place del la Revolution, where the guillotine held grim pride of place. Vendors in the crowds sold programs listing the schedule of executions taking place throughout the day. Many families brought children to witness the violent events. Famously, a group of Parisian knitting women became fixtures of the executions, watching and inciting the crowd. Executions were so frequent that Jacobin Louis Saint Just stated with satisfaction, "The ship of the revolution can only arrive safely at its destination on a sea that is red with torrents of blood."

One of the victims of this period of terror was Marie Antoinette herself. On October 14, 1793, nine months after the death of her husband, she was put on trial for treason. Other charges were also brought against the former queen, including the accusation that she had been abusing her young son, the dauphin. She was convicted of all charges and condemned to death on October 15th and executed by guillotine the following day. Unlike with King Louis the XVI, who had been transported in a private, closed carriage and allowed some dignity, the Queen was paraded through the streets in an open tumbrel cart, as any other condemned criminal would be.

This terrible period ended when Robespierre lost favor with other members of the Committee of Public Safety. The discontent seemed magnified by his over- reaching into matters of faith after having de-Christianized France. The Cult of the Supreme Being he proposed as a national religion in place of Catholicism was based on his own vision of a deist faith. The accompanying celebration, the Festival of the Supreme Being, which took place on June 8th saw Robespierre in the self-styled role of leader of the people. He was described as appearing as Moses come down from the mountain with the Ten Commandments. One of his colleagues accused, "It's not enough for him to be master, he has to be God." This entire performance led to the belief that Robespierre was attempting to set himself as the deity in his own new religion and gain a whole new level of power and influence.

Robespierre gave a speech in July 1794 warning that there were enemies of the Revolution within the Convention who had not yet been identified and were actively plotting a conspiracy against the Republic. When Robespierre pointedly did not name these enemies, his former allies feared he was about to call for their executions. Reacting quickly, they arrested him for crimes against the Republic. He was shot in the mouth during his arrest, either by his own hand or by one of his attackers, General de brigade Charles Andre Merda. He was taken into custody and laid out on a table in the room of the Committee of Public Safety, where he bled from his wound until it was bound up in a handkerchief. The following day, he was brought to the Place de Revolution to be executed without a trial under the rule of the recently approved decree of 22 Prairial, which Robespierre himself had helped to pass in the Committee of Public Safety. In his grim final moments, as the executioner positioned his neck in the frame, the bandage around his jaw was torn free. This sudden displacement caused Robespierre to scream in pain and fall silent with the fall of the blade.

Chapter Ten

The Last Revolutionaries

"History is the version of past events that people have decided to agree upon."

—Napoleon Bonaparte

After the Reign of Terror, the governing body of France once again found itself in a state of upheaval. The King and Queen were dead and the monarchy dissolved. The Girondin and Jacobin parties had been decimated by the guillotine. The citizens were still reeling from the explosion of violence and fear under the Reign of Terror. The Legislative Assembly was renamed the National Convention, distancing the new group from the horrors so recently committed under the rule of the Legislative Assembly and Robespierre's elite group, the Committee of Public Safety.

On the positive side, although the country continued to war with her neighbors, the French army now met with unprecedented success. By the spring of 1795, France had been victorious against the allied forces of the coalition on every front. The French army had pushed into territories around Amsterdam and the Rhine, and even into the Pyrenees. Prussia, one of the first nations to take up arms against France, had been forced to leave the coalition and already signed a separate peace treaty with France. With the French army threatening coalition positions in northern Italy, General Napoleon Bonaparte was given command.

Napoleon was able to force Austrian and Sardinian forces in Italy to sign the treaty of Campo Formio ceding the Austrian Netherlands to France and creating the Cisalpine and Ligurian republics in Italy. This success was followed by the establishment of republican regimes in Rome, Switzerland, and the Italian Piedmont. Unfortunately for France, Napoleon's string of successes would end when Admiral Nelson and the British fleet destroyed the French navy in Egypt at the Battle of the Nile.

While the military expanded French territories, the National Convention approved a new constitution for the nation, creating a bicameral legislature for the first time in France's history. Main executive power was granted to a five-member group called the Directory. This change was unpopular with royalists and revolutionaries alike, but their opposition was quickly ended when the French military under the command of general Napoleon Bonaparte, recently returned from campaigns in Egypt, acted in support of the Directory. The military continued to gain influence in the government as the Directory granted more and more power to the generals in the field, as it was clear the Directory would fall without their constant support. On November 9, 1799, Napoleon arranged for the Councils to take refuge in the suburban Chateau de Saint Cloud from a non-existent Jacobin plot.

With the Councils safely out of the way, Napoleon staged a coup d'état that resulted in the abolishment of the Directory and the establishment of the Consulate. Napoleon would soon appoint himself as first consul of France, and with his troops occupying the city, he was unopposed. The Revolution was over and there was no longer any danger of interference from foreign powers in France's new government. The victory of the French army over Austria in 1800 ending in the Treaty of Luneville left only Britain in the coalition against France. The Napoleonic era followed during which Napoleon's successful military campaigns saw France come to dominate much of Europe under his leadership.

Chapter Eleven

Legacy of the Revolution

"The modern tradition is the tradition of revolt. The French Revolution is still our model today: history is violent change, and this change goes by the name of progress."

—Octavio Paz

Although the French Revolutionary government, under its many names, only held power for a short time before being overtaken by Napoleon, this time of war, revolt, and internal turmoil is seen as one of the most important periods in world history. The final abolishing of the monarchy in France in favor of a government based on the will of the people was something new in the world. The antiquated system of feudalism was gone and replaced by individual free will and equality. Moreover, the Revolution opened opportunities for many who had traditionally been excluded for reasons of social status or faith. Society in France and other parts of Europe was forever changed. The ancient structure underlying the aristocracy's life of privilege could never be rebuilt. Legal equality gradually became an accepted fact in most of Europe.

The French Revolution has been a guiding factor in world politics, as more and more nations turned toward governments based on equal rights and equal representation. Women gained equality and slavery was abolished. The events in France showed the world the power of the common people, as well as provided a lesson on the terrible lengths to which that power can be taken. The Reign of Terror should not and will not be soon forgotten, and neither will the spirit of the people who rose against tyranny and demanded liberty and equality as natural rights given to them by their Creator and not to be taken away by any human master.

In the words of Enlightenment philosopher Thomas Hobbes, "Men look not at the greatness of the evil past, but the greatness of the good to follow." Perhaps the terrible extremes to which the revolutionaries took for their desire for social change can be softened by the great progress that has been wrought with the passage of time.

Made in the USA
San Bernardino, CA
31 March 2019